LET'S-READ-AND-FIND-OUT SCIENCE®

STAGE 1

OUR
Puppies
ARE GROWING

by Carolyn Otto • illustrated by Mary Morgan

HarperCollins*Publishers*

For Midori, Phyllis, KZ, Skinner, and Megan
—C.O.

For my son Dylan
—M.M.

Special thanks to Father Christopher of the Monks of New Skete for his time and expert review.

The *Let's-Read-and-Find-Out Science* book series was originated by Dr. Franklyn M. Branley, Astronomer Emeritus and former Chairman of the American Museum–Hayden Planetarium, and was formerly co-edited by him and Dr. Roma Gans, Professor Emeritus of Childhood Education, Teachers College, Columbia University. Text and illustrations for each of the books in the series are checked for accuracy by an expert in the relevant field. For more information about Let's-Read-and-Find-Out Science books, write to HarperCollins Children's Books, 10 East 53rd Street, New York, NY 10022, or visit our web site at http://www.harperchildrens.com.

HarperCollins®, ☙®, and Let's Read-and-Find-Out Science® are trademarks of HarperCollins Publishers Inc.

Our Puppies Are Growing
Text copyright © 1998 by Carolyn Otto
Illustrations copyright © 1998 by Mary Morgan

Library of Congress Cataloging-in-Publication Data
Otto, Carolyn.
  Our puppies are growing / by Carolyn Otto ; illustrated by Mary Morgan.
    p.   cm. — (Let's-read-and-find-out science.   Stage 1)
  Summary: A dog's young owner describes the birth of her puppies and their first few weeks of life.
  ISBN 0-06-027271-6. — ISBN 0-06-027272-4 (lib. bdg.). — ISBN 0-06-445169-0 (pbk.)
  1. Puppies—Growth—Juvenile literature.   2. Dogs—Development—Juvenile literature.   [1. Dogs.   2. Animals—Infancy.]   I. Morgan-Vanroyen, Mary, 1957– ill.   II. Title.   III. Series.
SF426.5.O88   1998   97-27697
636.7'07—dc21   CIP
                                                                                                                       AC

Typography by Al Cetta
1 2 3 4 5 6 7 8 9 10
❖
First Edition

OUR
Puppies
ARE GROWING

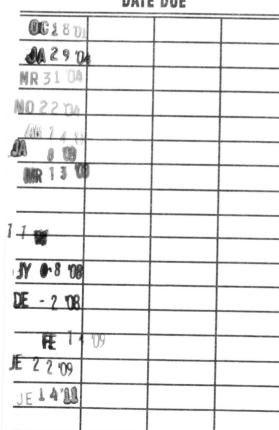

When I put my arms around our dog, she feels fatter than she used to. She has puppies growing inside her—more than one puppy, more than two, maybe three or four, maybe more.

I hold my ear against her belly, hoping to hear the puppies inside. I feel something bump and move, as if a puppy is turning over.

In the beginning, I couldn't believe there were puppies inside our dog. My brother says they start out small, too small to see, smaller than dust.

He shows me a picture in his book of little things that look like grains of rice. They are unborn puppies, only a few weeks old. In the next picture, a few weeks later, the things look like tiny fish.

As days go by and weeks go past, those fishy things grow and change until finally they look more like puppies. After nine weeks growing inside, puppies are big enough to be born.

I think I can't wait.
But I have to.

Embryo

When the first puppy is born at last, it looks like he's in a plastic bag. Our dog tears open the bag with her teeth. She licks the puppy over and over. She cleans the puppy with her tongue and nudges him softly with her nose.

The puppy moves. He starts to breathe.

And he's already hungry. Soon
he is drinking his mother's milk.
By my bedtime, we have
seven puppies—three girls
and four boys.

12

We weigh each of them on the kitchen scale, and my brother writes down the numbers. Then my father gently takes one puppy, and he dips her paws in a pan of food coloring. I help to make pawprints on a sheet of paper. Later, we'll see how much her feet grew.

In the morning, I go to the kitchen and stop just outside the doorway. Our dog is eating from her bowl, and the puppies are asleep in their box. I wait and watch until my mother tells me I can come in, and she gives me a puppy to hold. I cradle him in my arms. I'm very careful, and our dog doesn't mind.

The puppy wakes and sucks on my finger. He can't bite. He doesn't have teeth. He feels very small in my hands.

The puppy's eyes are tightly closed. He won't be able to see for a while. He can't hear yet, either. His ears are sealed shut inside. His legs are wobbly. He can't walk. When I put him down, he paddles along as if he's trying to swim.

For a week, the puppies sleep and eat and sleep and sleep and sleep. I draw a picture of them sleeping all tumbled together to stay warm.

It's hard to tell the puppies apart. They have big heads and tiny bodies.

One day, a puppy opens her eyes, and she blinks at my brother and me. It's been almost two weeks. She still can't see very well. She doesn't even notice us. She goes back to sleep right away.

After three weeks, the puppies are bigger. They weigh a lot more than they did. They can see me. And their ears have opened to sound. The puppies hear my footsteps and my voice. They can bark. They walk and run, and they can wag their tails.

We are teaching the puppies to eat. It's fun but really messy. My brother dabs cottage cheese on their faces, and the puppies lick it off.

Once the puppies can eat and drink by themselves, our dog won't have to feed them so much.

The puppies are six and a half weeks old today, and they are chewing on everything. They have sharp new baby teeth. Now that they can eat solid food, our dog doesn't need to feed them. But they still like to snuggle.

In a week or two, the puppies will be
ready for other homes. But our favorite will
stay with us. My brother and I will look
after her. We'll play tag and ball. We'll keep
her. We'll watch her grow.

If your dog has puppies, you will find out that being a mother is not easy. Newborn puppies are helpless, and your dog must feed them, keep them clean and warm, and protect them from harm.

When you want to see the puppies or handle them, be calm and very gentle. Make sure you are not upsetting their mother. The first few times you visit the puppies, it's best to be with a grown-up.

To hold a puppy, fold your arms in the shape of a cradle. One arm will support the puppy's chest and front legs, and the other arm supports the rear.

It takes more than a year for a puppy to grow into an adult dog. But a year passes quickly. Whether your dog is having puppies or you are bringing a new puppy home, it's a good idea to keep a scrapbook. You can note weight gain and growth or the things a puppy learns. You may want to include pictures and photographs, or pawprints made with food coloring.

Just see how much this puppy's feet grew!

Find Out More About PUPPIES

1. If you are lucky enough to have a new puppy, make a "baby book" to help you remember what it was like as it grows. Keep photos and drawings of your pet, along with short stories of funny things your pet has done.

2. Weigh your pet on the first day of every month. Ask an adult to help you make a graph to show your puppy's growth. If your parents have a graph of your weight gain when you were a baby, compare how babies and puppies grow.

3. Everybody loves to take pictures of their pets! Ask your relatives, friends, and neighbors to show you pictures of their pets when the pets were young. Make a "before and after" comparison. See how much or how little they changed.

4. Dogs come in lots of varieties or breeds. Cut out magazine pictures of all the different kinds of dogs you can find. Make a scrapbook. Which breeds do your friends and neighbors like best? Take a survey to find out. Show your scrapbook to different people; then make a chart to show which breeds are most popular.

5. Make a list of all the different animals that you see in a day. At night, think of ways to classify the animals. Can they be divided into different groups? Think about:

    where they live (indoors or outdoors);

    what kinds of body coverings they have (fur or feathers or scales, etc.);

    how they move (walk and run or swim or fly).

6. Think about the names that people give their dogs. Can you put the names into groups (funny names, people names, names that describe how the dog looks, etc.)?

7. Make up a story called "Me as a Puppy" to tell what you would do all day long if you were a dog!

8. Did you know that pets are good for people's health? Interview people that you know who have pets. Do they think that pets keep them happy and healthy?

9. Talk to people who take care of dogs or other animals for a living. You might like to meet a veterinarian, a zookeeper, or a dog breeder. Why did they choose this kind of a job? What do they like most about their jobs? What do they wish people would do for animals?

10. Most animals lay eggs and leave them to hatch and grow up on their own. Few animals care for their young until they are able to take care of themselves. How are mother dogs like human parents? Make a list of all the things your parents did for you that you can now do all by yourself.

11. Our pet dogs are descended from animals that had to hunt and fight for food. You can see that your puppy still has some of these instincts. Make a pull toy by knotting an old rag. Play tug-of-war with your puppy to find out if he still has some hunter instincts!